ALSO BY SHANE McCRAE

/

MULE

BLOOD

FORGIVENESS FORGIVENESS

THE ANIMAL TOO BIG TO KILL

IN THE LANGUAGE OF MY CAPTOR

THE GILDED AUCTION BLOCK

SOMETIMES I NEVER SUFFERED

CAIN NAMED THE ANIMAL

THE MANY HUNDREDS OF THE SCENT

NEW AND COLLECTED HELL

FARRAR STRAUS GIROUX / NEW YORK

NEW AND COLLECTED HELL

/

A POEM

/

SHANE McCRAE

Farrar, Straus and Giroux
120 Broadway, New York 10271

Library of Congress Cataloging-in-Publication Data
Names: McCrae, Shane, 1975- author.
Title: New and collected hell : a poem / Shane McCrae.
Description: First edition. | New York : Farrar, Straus and Giroux, 2025.
Identifiers: LCCN 2024034090 | ISBN 9780374615499 (hardcover)
Subjects: LCSH: Hell—Poetry. | LCGFT: Poetry.
Classification: LCC PS3613.C385747 N49 2025 | DDC 811/.6—dc23/eng/20240729
LC record available at https://lccn.loc.gov/2024034090

Designed by Crisis

Our books may be purchased in bulk for promotional,
educational, or business use. Please contact your local
bookseller or the Macmillan Corporate and Premium
Sales Department at 1-800-221-7945, extension 5442, or
by email at MacmillanSpecialMarkets@macmillan.com.

www.fsgbooks.com
Follow us on social media at @fsgbooks

10 9 8 7 6 5 4 3 2 1

For Michael, and always for Melissa

*If one can believe the book
of symbols.*

—DANA LEVIN

Note: Several of the previously collected poems have been revised toward the coherence of the whole, and where I thought I could improve the poems, I have attempted to do so.

CONTENTS

Invocation 3

The Hell Poem

The Hell Poem 7

The Hell Poem DLC

The Reformation 41

The Finger and the Ditch 49

Interlude: The Mind of Hell 54

Interlude: Law Converges on Itself 56

A Backward Well 61

A Revelation of a Further Darkness 64

No One Goes in Whole or Comes out Healed 65

I squeezed through 68

Law's Dream 71

The Dream at the End of the Dream 79

Acknowledgments 91

NEW AND COLLECTED HELL

Invocation

Of death the muse is death the muse of Hell
Is death the muse   of Heaven I don't know
O   muse of where how   can I hope to go
To where I pray I'll go   sing at least   tell
Muse I can't name who   knew the first who fell
Maybe or never met him coming so
Long after even his stink was gone and low
Too far to catch   but sing   the flesh-hot cell
And hotter than and colder than and blood
-ier as if it were   the XL ink
Cartridge from which all flesh is printed   sing
Hell   and the one who breathless wandering
Stumbled through once   and anything you think
Might make strange justice a familiar good

THE
HELL
POEM

The Hell Poem

Then Chukwu saw the people's souls in birds
Coming towards him like black spots off the sunset
To a place where there would be neither roosts nor trees
Nor any way back to the house of life.

—SEAMUS HEANEY

1. Intake Interview

Describe the lake I'm still
        not   sure
                how I got here I was just   hiking
                Or not exactly
        hiking but
I like to walk in the woods   behind
My house I mean
        my   apartment
                in the woods behind the complex so
                I'm hiking
        it's a nice day sure a little
hot I guess but there's
A nice breeze so   I'm hiking
        up this hill and I
                start to get really
                Hot and I
        can't breathe but I
just   need   maybe to rest for just
A minute I
        look for a bench a rock for
                something but I can't
                See anywhere to sit
        and now I have to sit I   think I'll
faint
Then suddenly I'm rowing I'm

surrounded now

          by sailboats nice

          Boats yachts I guess I mean

     that's just a big boat

right white   yachts and sail

 boats and I'm rowing this

     it's small an open

          boat I'm rowing but

          It's like I'm on a track

     the waves don't

rock my boat   and I stop rowing

But I don't slow down

     plus I'm   invisible this yacht

          it's drifting

          Looks like it's drifting and it slams

     into me I mean *BANG*

I thought

I would die

     but it bounces off

          the people on the yacht they all

          Looked like that one

     rich guy on *Gilligan's*

Island well they don't hear it

Don't even flinch

     it's like they're on   tracks on the yacht

          it's like they're robots

          At Chuck E. Cheese and

     me it's like

I'm in a bubble on a track

Too I'm fine

        I don't feel a thing

                so now of course I'm terrified

                Describe   *the bird* the bird

      the bird

looked like a big   gray seagull but

The bird looked like a robot too

      but free   the bird looked free

          it dove

          And landed in the boat at my

     feet in between my feet

and spoke

It sounded like a dog

      barking it

          sounded like it couldn't speak

          It said

      barking it said *Hey*   *fuck you*

fucking   *shithead follow me*

And coughed this little toy

      skeleton hand up

          middle finger up

          And then it took off

      barking

and the bird looked free it couldn't have

Been free   if I was stuck

     and followed it

          stuck on a track   or maybe

          The bird was free but everybody

     has a boss

I let the oars slip
Into the lake
           except they didn't   sink they just
                        stood there   then heads
                        And necks and faces
           sprouted from the handles then
arms and legs sprouted
From the sides   and the oars walked away *Describe*
           the oars
                        they walked on water
                        Like oars
           their faces steamed in the sun
and the steam caught the light from the sun
And glowed above their heads they
           walked   away
                        from where the boat was going
                        Describe the gate the boat kept going
           toward this weird
whirlpool in the middle
Of the lake it was
           I mean the water looked
                        pixelated white but splotchy
                        And it   the water swirled
           pixel by pixel from
pixel to pixel
It looked like it would hurt to fall in
           they   the pixels looked
                        like churning
                        Teeth and that's where the boat

                    took me the gate
chewed it to splinters and
As the boat broke
                and sank I looked
                                down and saw I   was floating level
                                With the surface of the lake
                and the lake
on all sides was disappearing
Fading and I saw night
                beneath me
                                for a moment I was   any
                                -one watching from   above me would have
                seen a bright
spot in a darkness
I must have been
                I must have looked
                                exactly like   if only then
                                The man I always thought I was
                high above Hell
and then I fell

2a. The Fall / The Tyrant Beetle at the Banks of the Living River of the Dead

I fell a whole   lifetime of fall
-ing as I fell   and as I fell I
Fell through my life I watched my life

Projected   on the walls of the hole
I fell through but projected through
No lens no carried by no light

No but projected   like a movie
On the walls of the hole I fell through but
Backward like   watching was like watching

A movie from behind the screen
In kind of it was   in black and white   but
In supersaturated whites

And blacks like scraps   of carbon paper
Their edges spilling over the edges
Of the darknesses in the world the blacks and

Whites overflowed the objects they
Belonged to the objects   I had thought
Belonged to them   and as I watched

Falling   the camera overflowed
The edges of my memories
Once   and again and then again

To follow people I had hurt
Through selfishness   through inattention
From the edges of my memories

Into their memories I saw
Falling the harm I did   I saw
Eventually I   even my

Harm   disappeared I disappeared I
Had thought   at least the scars I made
Would be the scars I made forever

Until I wasn't I   just   stopped
Falling suddenly and no impact
Suddenly I'm   standing in
A room my back against   it feels
Like skin a wall but   only as long as
It takes for me to realize
I'm standing in a room my back
Against a wall   and the wall oppo
-site from me disappears the wall
Behind me slides   forward and shoves
Me out of the room I stumble into
A cave or warehouse somewhere big
And dark that didn't really feel like

Part of the world   facing a row
Of mumbling kneeling   corpses their
Eyes open their mouths   closed but mum
-bling but the mumbling   voices didn't
The sounds of the voices didn't come
From them the voices   flooded from
A giant black   hundred-legged beetle
Hovering in front of and above
The corpses its black back to me its
Pale orange belly   pulsing from
Each leg a different voice poured and
As I stepped near   it spoke to me
But somehow only in my head
Look at me   I'm a huge   success   you
Want to know how I got to be where
I am   of course you do   of course
You do   see this   tremendous line
Of people here   I promise you
Trust me   ok   you will not find
A more tremendous group of people
Anywhere   ok   and they're all waiting
For me   just to hear what I'll say
Ok   and they don't know   can you
Believe it   they've already heard it
You're hearing it right now   believe me
It might not sound like much   but when
I'm all you hear   and all you see
I'm everything the   beetle's voice
Swallowed my mind consumed me I

Staggered to one   end of the row
And knelt and as I knelt a man
At the other   end of the row stood
And walked   into the dark beyond it
Opening and closing his
Mouth   like a goldfish what   I think
Breathing   or like a cartoon shark
Chasing a goldfish really just
Snapping its jaws its fat shark head
Stuck in the bowl   and disappeared
Into the dark beyond the corpses
Talking   out loud his body dis
-appeared   but as his body faded
His voice detached from the beetle and
Became his voice again which I
Had never known to be his voice
And as his body disappeared
His voice grew stronger and I heard
Him call my name   and stood   my voice
By then had nearly left my thoughts
As when a cartoon scientist must
Enter a sick friend's body in
A specially built submarine
That shrinks and is herself shrunk down
To microscopic size her voice
Shrinks and becomes a squeaking noise my
Voice had become a squeaking noise
Behind the sniffing   wheedling noise
That was the beetle's   actual voice

I stood   and gasping staggered into
The darkness past the corpses   there I
Saw the man who   had risen and walked
And who as waves   are freed and roll
Across a tub   only to break
Against the belly of the man
Who freed them climbing in   the man who
Had risen was free   only to walk
From one oblivion to another
From noise to all I saw   was empty
Darkness   and I followed him
But caught him only after we
Had walked too far to hear the voices
Although the beetle's orange belly
Still pulsed in the distance like a turning
Lighthouse beam   or a house burning
On a far shore   the moment we
Stepped beyond the noise horizon
The man stopped short   I following
Too close and reaching   out just then
To tap his shoulder stumbled and
Fell into him   and the man fell
First to his knees then   forward onto
His face without   raising his arms
To stop himself   among the dead I
Mistook the dead for the living and
Afraid he might be hurt   I crouched
And rolled him over   and he spoke then
I didn't   call your name I just

Said it out loud I just   it had
Become my name the moment you
Knelt I just   wanted to hear it
I wasn't   asking you to follow
Me   the river   was the river
Lethe the dead forget their lives there
As eddies in the ever-changing
Living river of the dead   I
Left it to find my Hell   I don't
Know what I did to earn my place
In Hell   I took your name   as mine
Was taken long before you came
I couldn't   when my name was taken
I couldn't rise to follow it
How did you rise to follow me

Before I had a chance to answer
I heard the sound of hammers striking
Metal and raised   my eyes to look
And in the once-empty darkness there
Before us now I saw a huge
White factory and floodlights most
Trained on the factory and one
Sweeping the field surrounding it
And in that light the man who fell
Vanished he vanished as the beam
Swept the black ground before me asking
Again *How did you rise*   the beam

Swept past me stopped   swept back and stopped and
Fixed on me   first yellow   then orange
Then red then light and heat combined
The heat that had been   weaker than
The orange light it now the heat was
Equal to the light the red light dimmed and
The heat increased the factory's
Enormous rolling door rolled open

2b. The Angel of the Body

And two human   -shaped shapes emerged
From the dark inside   and called my name

I almost didn't answer them
I turned   but found the field behind
Me gone I found a wall behind me
Made of red pulsing   blocks it rose
Into the sky or   rose to where
If there had been a sky the sky
Would have been rose   as high and past
Where it that sky it would have ended
I swallowed tasted   blood I answered
The hammers stopped   the red wall dis
-appeared a high-pitched *Whoop Whoop Whoop*
Rushed I turned back to look   from the fac
-tory I couldn't see the source
I ran   my footfalls echoed first
One echo for each footfall then
A second then a third the echoes
Slipping out   of phase with the sounds
I made   and overhead I heard
Wingbeats and *Whoop Whoop Whoop* the light
From the beetle's belly as I got
Closer retreated as I got
Closer the light   changed from orange

To red and as the light retreated
The heat increased   until the light
Was a small dot on the horizon
And the heat was unbearable

And then the echoes stopped   and I
Stopped running *You   don't choose to run*
I choose to make you run it was
A small child's voice behind me shouting
I choose to drive you closer to
The fire you hope will rescue you
The wings you heard were my wings beating
The feet you heard were my feet running
I am a many in a one
Hunting I join the sky to the earth
As hunting I join life to death
And stand between them   like a dam
Between a river and a lake
I called your name from the gate of the city
I   was chasing you before
You answered turn   and face me   yes
Why do you cringe and cower aren't
You dead   already aren't you damned
Already but   perhaps you love
It still that   prize you call your body
You can't   love it here you   can't own it
Here   and what else has your love been
What hasn't your love claimed   you need
-n't fear   to lose that love you will

Lose nothing but the great delusion
That brought you here   you will be free
You won't be   subject to the vicious
Whims of that body   which because
You didn't recognize it was
A mind was stronger than your mind
Be glad   here   let me help you root
Your love out   have you felt around
For it I'll show you where to look

The demon   who had spoken from
Behind me   first now rose from the dirt
In front of me four   legs four arms
Four wings   two heads the same   child's face twice
And twenty fingers   twenty claws
They plowed a claw across my chest
And reached inside the   robot bird
Alighted then   on the demon's shoulder

And as my vision darkened as I
Lost consciousness   spat   and barked *You're*
So fucking stupid I can't stand it

At that a darkness like the darkness
Before the world was overtook me

3a. In a Dream the Robot Bird
Tells Me How It Is I Am in Hell

I dreamed I lay at the feet of the demon
Child twitching and   the robot fluttered
Down from their shoulder   kicked me hard
And growling whispered in my ear

My name is Law   I do the work
The boss says he   created me in
The   in the however long it was
Between when Cain crushed Abel's fore

-head with a rock   and the first drop of
Blood hit the ground   I was the voice
Of the blood crying out to God
You know   the thing in the Bible   God says

The voice of thy   brother's blood crieth
Unto me from the ground *that shit*
Happened   I was a baby all fucking
Bawling and shit   yeah   anyway

I say that makes   Cain killing Abel
I say that makes   Abel poor dickless
Abel the   first human and
The father of all humankind

But the boss he says different
He says it's him   the boss   for making
The murder possible and he's
Not   philosophical like me

He doesn't have to be but he
Is sure as shit he's   fucking   he's
Smarter than me   smarter than you
Anyway so   listen   a couple

Weeks ago we got a fax
You think there'd be   a phone in Hell
Fuck no   we fax   so anyway
We got a fax   about you shit

-For-brains it said you   would be coming
Down and the boss wanted you
To get a tour   at first I thought
It meant the boss down here because   you

Know   he's the boss I think things mean
But then I heard him   shouting and
Breaking shit   in the throne room and
I realized   it meant the boss boss

And as this dawns on me he   stomps
Out of the throne room sees the I
Don't know the joy of knowing what's
Going on for once flash in my eyes

Or some shit and he's fucking pissed
Next thing I know I'm guiding your
Slow ass through Hell   but the boss doesn't
Want you to know you're getting special

Treatment so if you see him   keep your
Mouth shut oh shit   how will you breathe
Fuck you I know you're just pretending
To breathe   that shit still works   you dumbass

So back to Abel   what I think is
If Abel's not your father Cain
Is after   all he had the big
Rock   and how many times you think

He saw his dad kill anything by
Crushing its head not   many right
Nah man an arrow in the heart
And by the way that's what God gave you

By telling Adam he could name
The animals   God told you where
Their hearts were   Adam never missed
A shot   you think that sounds like bullshit

But he was using a gift God
Had given him   so killing was
Like prayer for him   but Cain   he looked
Abel in the eyes   and saw himself

Not in his brother's heart   but in
His head   and crushed his head   and yeah
Where else do humans start   Cain named
The animal in Abel's head

3b. In a Dream I Glimpse
the Burning Edge of Heaven

I dreamed I was alive I dreamed
In Hell I woke dreamed waking on
A mountainside   I dreamed I woke
But in the dream I also dreamed I
Had been awake   for years on the mountain
I dreamed the bird had brought me there
I dreamed the bird had carried me
To the mountain from   between my first
Death and a second death it said
It couldn't stand to watch I dreamed
I rested on the mountainside
Cross-legged and   for years the bird
Had come and gone   many times come
And gone and it had mentioned many
Times a test I might   not recog
-nizing it fail   and though the bird had
Threatened and tried   to bribe me with
More life I hadn't risen   at
Those times I watched   pine trees at the foot
Of the mountain inch   toward the mountain
Then back again each breathing and
Breathed by the mountain every living
Thing on the mountain   moved as if
Breathed by the mountain   in and out

I saw more clearly as I rested
Everything moving   back and forth
Until the sun itself as slowly
As it moved   seemed to be a part
Of the motion   in and out   and back
And forth   so that I saw it even
In the night   moving on the other side
Of the world so that I saw the darkness
Deepening as the sun drew closer
To the spot on the other side
Of the world   farthest from the mountain
And from the moment the sun left
That spot I saw the morning coming
In the changing blackness of the sky

For years I sat on the mountainside
And watched the bird fly silently
Across the sky   from south to north
Or what I thought was south to north
And as it always   as it flew
To the north it crossed between the sun
And me at the zenith of the course
Of the sun across the sky   and al
-ways as it flew to the south it crossed
My zenith just   as the sun disap
-peared over the horizon for
Years I watched and after years
I saw the bird begin to change
I saw the bird begin to fade

I saw and watched it   silently
At first the bird   looked like an image
Moving across an image burned
Into a monitor   but soon
The bird looked   like an image burned
Into a monitor   but moving
Behind the image in the foreground
And then as I was watching it
One afternoon or morning as
It crossed the sun the sunlight burning
Through it I   was blinded for
A moment   and when I could see
Again the bird was gone   I searched
The sky   and searching realized
The sun was still   the distant clouds
Were still and I glanced down and saw
Only the pines at the foot of the mountain
Moving the pines at the foot of the mountain
Began to climb toward me

                              I dreamed
They climbed   faster than any living
Being could climb   as if they were
Not bound by life to the world they lived in
And darkened as they climbed   and their
Dark needles as they climbed glowed   red
And redder and   when they had almost
Reached me the bird emerged from them
And flew ahead   and turned its back to
Me and the bird spoke then   to the pines

It spoke a language I had never
Heard it sounded speaking like
Wind in pine needles the trees spoke back
They spoke   a different language back
Their language sounded like a bird's
Wings flapping as it leaves a tree
But I could see they understood
Each other and   the pines stopped climbing
Their needles faded   they turned back
And climbed down slowly the bird watched
Them silently they made it half
-way back   down to the foot of the mountain

Then   the dream changed the sun slipped down
To the edge of the sky the sky itself
Even before the sun set went
Black and the pines ignited burn
-ing needles flew   from the pines in all
Directions the   pines burning looked like
Sparklers throwing off slow wander
-ing sparks then   the sky opened as
The sky would open or a U
FO would open in the sky
To take a soul   to take a person
Away   but all it took was fire
The flames grew taller seemed to stretch
Taller to reach the hole in the sky
They rose   and rising they released
The pines and now and the pines stood dead
The bird   who had until now watched them

Shifting its weight   from foot to foot
Now turned to me   and barking asked
Why fucking don't you fucking   go   oh
Shit   shit I've seen that look before
Shit even this   even   Hell you think it's
OK   shit   you   you know   I've been
Watching you since before you fucks
Knew you were you   you know what makes you
Monsters   a human is the on
-ly creature that can fatten con
-suming itself it's   Hell it's fucking
HELL and the bird it was   shaking lunged
At me it tried to lunge but could
-n't but it   as if it were chained
At the ankle to a peg in the dirt
Snapped back and almost   fell and then
Shaking it tried   to fly it leaped
Flapping its wings they sounded like
Chains   the bird fell   down facedown screaming
In the dirt hot light   burst from its back   that
Light not the screams   woke me that sound
-ed like a world of screams   I heard
The screaming world   and still I dreamed

4. A Face

I woke in light in dirt
In a road   healed in what
Looked like an old west ghost town
The kneeling corpses kneeling

At the edge of the town
Facing away   the robot
Bird circled overhead
Then seeing I had woken

Landed beside me opened
Its gray beak wide   and barked
And spoke   *Before am was*
I am   and sought to be

I am and seek to be
And seeking I made you
And all your kind   your kind
My child   for surely mine

My child   for surely mine
My child Hold on a sec
This fucking thing   it always
Sticks fuck him the useless

Fuck and the robot bird
Unfurled its metal wings
Took off   and threw itself
Into a pillar growling

That ought to   fucking do
It then   the other voice
The human voice inside
The robot bird's breast shouted

MY CHILD   for surely mine
Best born if not the first
You are   Death came before
And bears the imperfections

Of a first draft my   child
I seek and I have sought
From the beginning to
Help you to grow   if I

Have not seemed nurturing
Know I have striven none
-theless to attend to our
Relationship and would

Not choose if I could choose
To be ignored   Love binds us
Through   I acknowledge   com
-plications but the more

Tangled the knot the strong
-er the knot holds   beloved
I welcome you to Hell
As a new mother welcomes

Her child to its life and body
And fear I must apol
-ogize for both   I made
You what you are   death-seeking

Out of pity for
My son   Death   who before
You couldn't find a job
But surely there are worse

Reasons for being   haven't
You often wished you knew
Whether you were conceived with
Love   for love's need   you were

My child you were   and serve
A purpose   you are Hell
Its living walls   its rivers
You are each other's flames

In life and in this life
And you will find yourself
Unchanged   but would you know
Yourself if you weren't burning

I see your crime was love
You loved the world   and wanted
That love to end your ob
-ligations to the world

Why make the world   a garden
If you would punish its
Keeper for loving it   as
A father loves his wife

Here you will   be the world I
Grant you a part in it
Forever   I grant my wish
For you   to you   at last

You are what you were made for
And more so what you make
Employment and a home
For the god at the end of the world

Then the bird closed its beak
And turned its back to me
And darkness spread across
The ceiling   but the bird

Instead of leaping it
Had spread its wings and crouched
To leap instead of leaping
It paused   then stood again

And then turned back to me
And barked *Same speech*   *for I*
Don't fucking know how long
Five thousand years   *I mean*

Five thousand years ago   *sure*
Death was the god at the end
Of the world   *but now*   *nah*   *now*
Death's just the caterer

After a big-ass party
No   *it's you shits now*
You know   *the boss was there*
At the beginning of

The world you wanna know what
God said   *what words God spoke to*
Call humans into being
The boss says God said Snails

Make shells   *humans make hells*
And winked and there you were
And there was Hell beneath you
A face beneath a heel

But the boss lies a lot
Then   the bird turned again
And flew   toward the dark
Ceiling and even   as it

                                        Filled the darkness   it dis
                          -appeared in the darkness   like
            Paper burned loose from the kindling
            And flying from the fire

THE
HELL
POEM
DLC

The Reformation

1.

In the morning what I took
To be the morning   light
Burned through the ceiling sun
-light through a magnifying

Glass through paper but
It looked like a film melt
-ing a   consuming hole
The robot bird flew down

From the ceiling   landed on
My head bent   its head down
And whispered in my ear
Wake up you   fucker all

Night I had stood awake   un
-able to move all night but
As soon as the bird spoke I
Collapsed   the robot hovered

Where my head had been
And barked *Hurry   the fuck*
Up follow me   and turned and
Flew toward a fissure wid

-ening in the fleshy wall
At first it flew in silence
In front of and above me
Guiding me through a narrow

Tall cave   but after we e
-merged into a large chamber
The robot bird transformed
Like Starscream   really like

Any Decepticon
Any Transformer really
Except without the whirring
Into a giant human

-oid robot well   at least
A really tall one eight
Feet tall   at least and gray and
Its arms and legs were thin

As pencils slivers of
What looked like bone   white bone
Jutted from its knuckles
Gray like the parts of cars

You're not supposed to see
Stained with old blood   that rust   red
Color except it's oily
You sometimes see in splotches

On new car parts   in splotches
On the robot too   and stood still
Beside me for a moment
Facing a wide dark pit

In the middle of the chamber
Like an Olympic diver
Standing at the edge of the board
Her gaze fixed neither on

The pool nor any object
In the arena but
Inward instead her eyes
Now signs   now metaphors

Of and for visions no
Spectator could imagine
Before she leaps and leaping
Both transcends and makes

More definite the lim
-its of the human body
And then the robot growled
First stop's the HR bunker

Down at the bottom of
The-Pit-You-Cannot-See
-The-Bottom-Of's a mountain
We'll dive to the base   then climb

Up to the peak   from there
We'll take an elevator
Down to the center of
The mountain that's   the HR

Bunker the boss wants   if
The boss boss ever shuts
Us down   to have a record
He wants some evidence that

It was wrong to open Hell and
It's wrong to shut it down
He knows he'll stand before
A judge someday   he needs

A top-notch HR team
At this the robot turned
To look me in the eyes
And I think saw confusion

Hollow them   since as
It stepped to the black edge
Of the pit it   barked *Fuck you*
You think you know what suffer

-ing is   you asshole if
I asked you what it was
You'd probably try to tell me
That's how I know you don't

Know shit   and then it dove
Into the pit and though
I had   followed the bird
Freely I hadn't been

Bound   after it had fallen
Maybe twenty feet
I felt a cord I couldn't
See   unraveling

Before me then I felt
A jolt and a hot sting
As the cord jerked me forward
Too hard and quickly and

Tore through me just above
My hips   I saw my legs
Fall then I realized
The rest of me was falling

After them and falling
Faster than they were
And I flipped upside down
And stretched   forward to catch them

And caught them by my belt
And gasping flipped myself
Over   and pulled my legs
Up by the belt blood   sticking

My hands to the belt   I bled
More when I pulled the halves
Together bled so much
I couldn't see the wound

2.

I landed on my feet my femurs
Snapped free at the hip   and exited
My body through my upper chest
One on each side and just below my
Shoulders each trailing innards streamers

Burst from a party popper see
-ing them I felt   no pain but like
A stranger to my body   I watched
My femurs rocket forward as
The rest of my bones liquefied   my

Eyes sinking in a puddle of
Myself   the right   femur I think
The right one it   flew maybe thirty
Feet before thudding wetly into
The dirt the left (I had been left

-Handed in life) had   slammed against
The back of the robot's neck   and stuck
A moment then slid wetly down
And touched the black   dirt the same in
-stant the right femur touched it *What*

The fuck the giant   robot barked as
It turned   rubbing its neck   to me
Asshole   *that's gonna leave a mark* as
It barked I felt a tightening
I knew   was the invisible

Cord I had felt   at the edge of the pit
Even though I had no body it
Tightened my   puddle like a drain
Tightening water   and I saw
My femurs flying back to me

And felt my insides hardening
And realized I was watching from
A solid head again   and watched my
Femurs reenter me through the holes in
My chest they   had made exiting

My body coming back together
Hurt like I would have thought it flying
Apart would hurt   and coming back
Together the   each part   the pro
-cess of it raised me to my feet

Even as my   feet were recon
-stituted I   flew into me
And even though I felt my bones
Straighten inside me even though
I felt my torso and legs merge

And saw it   still the sound of it
My wet   parts recombining sounded
Just like paint splattering   as if
My body I had been was shaped
By chaos hidden in the bone

The Finger and the Ditch

After my body splattered back together
Or it was   splattered back together by
A hand or force I couldn't see a love

I couldn't see   a cruelty re-nerving
My body for more suffering the robot
Bird rolling its   clattering shoulders barked

If you've got bones and nerves and blood in you
Why aren't you moving   and again I felt
The cord I couldn't see the   cord that bound

Me to the bird the   cord that only minutes
Before had severed where   it tugged me now
My upper body from my lower body

Tugging me forward   though the bird stood still
Tugging me forward   like the mechanism
In a tape measure   that erases as

It winds the tape back in   the thing the tape
Had been unwound to show   the cord had ripped me
Apart to show me   no escaping Hell

A love of the suffering of others put
Me back together love   stitched me together
With a steel needle like a bowling pin in

-visible just like the cord   just like the love
And the cord dragged me to the bird   I fell
In the dirt at the first tug and the cord dragged me

To the bird bouncing   a stone skipped on a lake
The puffs of dust the puffs of mist my body
Would make   if it were skipped across smooth water

I stopped at the bird's feet the robot's feet
And coughing raised myself my   palms on the dirt
First to one knee   then to my feet *You sure*

You still   got human lungs you fucking sound like
A coffee grinder   grinding sand one hard
Jerk at a time the robot barked the bird

Barked its beak opening and closing like
A plastic   head tyrannosaurus head on
A plastic stick   operated by a child

Who uses it to grab small objects objects
A foot and   a half farther from him than
Without the head its sharp-toothed small-toothed jaws he

Could reach   the robot barked then squinted barked
Fuck you then turned around but just   before
It turned it looked   as it had looked the morning

We met   on the blue calm sudden lake that was
The gate through which I dropped to Hell the robot
A gull   I first thought tumbled from the sky

As if it had been thrown   into my rowboat
From Heaven or so hard from Hell it seemed
To fly before it fell   it staggered as

It stood then squinted first   at the lake   then me
Coughed *Fuck you   follow me*   and flew off coughing
I couldn't choose   and followed it to Hell

Now the bird walked   I didn't try to choose
I followed it to the verge of the boiling mountain
That boiled as if it were a lake on fire

The surface of the mountain   the fir trees
That leaped and sank like drunks on headless bulls
The bodies only   also leaping sinking

Spirits that can't see Hell is riding them
And leap to buck it   thinking Hell is men
And sink beneath its weight   and leap again

The bulls beneath the firs   and rocks like boots
In snow   in the dirt and in the dirty snow
Maintained at the summit by enormous loud

Machines   so hot it melted almost as
Soon as they made it   the flesh-colored snow
They made   of infinite flesh tones no snow

-flake was the same   color as any other
Though they all melted and flowed down the mountain
Together   and collected in a ditch

At the verge   through which rolled plants that looked
Like tumbleweeds but red and made of veins
The water shivered as the mountain boiled

The ditch was narrow   I stepped back a few
Steps then I ran   the few steps forward and
I leaped across it   and the mountain boiled

More furiously and the stream of flesh
-Toned water flowing from the peak at once
Flooded its banks and all the mountainside

At once was covered and the mountainside
At once became a face   but featureless
And sweating off its skin   and I stood ankle

-Deep in the skin   and turned to the robot bird
Who hadn't leaped   who barked before I spoke
What did you think would happen asshole who

Told you to jump the ditch the bird had been
Tugging the middle finger on its left
Hand as it barked   and now it bit the finger

Off   frowned and spat the finger in the ditch
And the red rolling plants in the ditch turned blue
And seemed to die   stopped rolling and just drifted

In the shallowing tan water as the water
Retreated from the face of the mountain and
Became again a stream of melted skin

Trickling down the mountain   and the bird
Then stepped across the ditch *You gotta pay*
Fucker or somebody is gonna have to

Pay for you you're   lucky that finger was
Worth ten of you the water   where the finger
Had entered chased the finger as it sank

Making a whirlpool where the finger sank
That slowly widened it   looked like a hole
In skin   bloodless   but opening forever

That would if it kept   growing would in time
Consume the ditch the mountain and all Hell
The bird stepped forward and began to climb

Interlude: The Mind of Hell

My ankles turn the mountain's sweat
Back rippling one   inch two with each
Step I take wading up the mountain
The brown sweat flowing down the mountain

Color of every skin tone merged
Eddies as if it were a mind
Of meat deciding   not a mind
Of liquid on a mountain whether

Deciding at my ankles whether
To turn   return to the sky-beached light
At the summit of the boiling mountain
The peak where no shade falls or gathers

To climb against the effortless
Fall to the summit   from which light
Is wrenched like water from a stone
By heat that vaporizes rock

Conflicting with the mind of Hell
That holds the rock together   where
The vapor and the willed rock meet
White light emerges   from there Hell

Is lit that is not everywhere
Lit   or to flow around my ankles
Down to the ditch at the base of the mountain
In which the new sweat would not raise

The level of the sweat already
Flowing but only thicken for
A moment only   slow the sweat
Consumed by uncontested heat

A mind of liquid seeming almost
To turn from being   liquid not to
Flow down but climb   as with each step
I take I tear the living sweat

And with each step I take it screams
But I have lived a human life
And step and step   and watch the sweat
For the shimmer I make tearing it

Interlude: Law Converges on Itself

With every step I wading up
                  The sweating mountain step
With every step I seem to sink
                  Deeper into the sweat

Until my All Stars disappear
                  Completely in the sweat
And glancing see no shadows where
                  The shadows of my shoes were

Unless I march my knees up high
                  Maybe   I march to check
And see a shoe slip   off I watch
                  Its shadow disappear

Too big to be its shadow step
                  The other shoe is gone
And though the sweat it   isn't rising
                  I can't now march my knees

Above the bright brown surface   in
                  The surface now I see
Standing its head too high above me
                  Law standing huge above me

Fucker you didn't give
Up shit to climb the mountain
And now the mountain's drinking you
You watched me tear my finger

Off and you didn't say
A word you didn't do
A thing you didn't give   up   shit
If I weren't bound to you

I wouldn't be here still
Asshole except   I wouldn't
For anything   miss what's about to
Happen Law blears away

Glowing and flattening and I
          I'm underwater under
Sweat   walking still not swept with the warm
               Sweat down the mountain shrinking

I must be shrinking but more slowly
          Now   and they were before
Invisible but now   I see
          Them   barely see them fading

In slowly first   as shapes but now
               Fish like those fish all mouth all
Teeth and too deep to see alive
               Dozens they see me seeing

Them and they all at   once they swim
                    At me the bigger eating
The smaller as they swim at me
                    Until there's only one

The biggest left its head as big
                    As mine not getting bigger
Its head its body mine is bigger
                    I'm slow but   dead I'm strong

It lunges I   raise my left arm
                    Across my face it bites
And sticks I panic shake my arm
                    It tumbles off a long

Fang breaking   off I pull the fang
                    Out of my arm no blood
The fang   is longer than the fish
                    I grip it like a knife

The fish again but now   more slowly
                    Lunges I jump to the side
And twist and stab connect I pull
                    The fang out stab again

Down hard and pin the fish to the sweating
                    Face of the mountain   it
Wriggles   no blood   gets smaller as
                    It wriggles disappears

I see Law's   feet in the sweat in front
                Of me I look up Law
Converges on itself I   rise
                To meet it dripping cold

Air stinging through the bloodless hole
                In my left arm the air
More painful than the bite was Law
                Looks at the hole and whistles

Except it no the whistle is
                It's a recording and
Law plays it twice   inside itself
                While leaning forward   looking

And then Law straightens   up and jumps
                And as it rises it
Becomes a bird again and as
                It rises   for an instant

I feel the cord that binds us tighten
                But then it disappears
That as I shrank had disappeared
                And Law flies down the mountain

Lands far away and pecks the sweat
                And lifts two shapes from the sweat
Then Law flies   back and drops my All
                Stars at my feet transforms

And lands ahead of me but facing

    The peak away I kneel

And tie my shoes the cord tears open

     My back when Law steps forward

A Backward Well

When Law it stood had climbed to   a step below the peak
Looked more a robot than had ever been a bird
It raised its right arm flicked its wrist   as if it were
Casting a lure   into a lake   and I again
Felt the invisible cord binding me to Law
Tighten around my waist   and all at once I stood
Not where I had been standing   thirty feet away
But right behind Law steps   from the peak of the mountain golden
Light from a source I couldn't see illuminated
Me half of me the third   from just below my heart
Up to my face   I couldn't see it shining on
My face   but knew the light was there because I couldn't
See   and I raised my hand to shade my eyes and even
Though now the brown   snow on the peak was visible
I couldn't see the source of the light no hovering orb
No glowing well   on the surface and light overflowing
But Law had stepped to the peak   and turned to me and barked
Well fucking step up asshole if you want to see it
'Cause you're not fucking gonna see it standing there
Nobody sees it who's not   standing on the peak
Come fucking on and so   I one step two steps stepped
To the peak of the mountain flat about   twelve feet across
Shaped like a pixelated circle at its center
A golden elevator   like an elevator
In a gray office building built in the '80s steel
-Gray but no building there   the elevator shone

Gold like a sunset on the ocean gold of that
Idea gold shining   but the brightness fading from
The gold like money fading from a desperate scheme
The final   notice in your hand but you could sell
Your clothes but you've already sold your good clothes Law
Frowned   barked *We call that elevator Golden Bough*
It is a golden   nail it was hammered through the mountain
Down to the HR bunker by the hand of the Devil
Himself his calloused palm   you don't deserve to bask
In the fucking glory of his works   he is a god who
Works   with his hands   his body   such a god makes gold
-en things   a god who works with words makes empty air
And worlds of dirt and muddy fire   and pushed the glowing
Button beneath the upside-down black triangle
So black I couldn't see it only   absence from
Which light could not escape   to the right of the golden door
To the right of the button on the side of the elevator
A panel opened and a man rolled out one roll
Two rolls   to the right of the elevator then he popped
To his feet   wearing nothing but a diaper and
A bellhop cap his skin   more scabs than skin   he bent
At his waist delicately like a man requesting
A dance in a Jane Austen movie   toward the panel
From which he had just rolled   his red scabs bursting then
Opened a smaller   inner panel and unfolded
Two cranks one   painted red the other red from heat
And first he turned the painted crank   the golden doors
Of the elevator slowly jerked apart   the crank
Grinding and fighting   him until the doors were all
The way apart   immediately he removed

His bellhop cap and rang a silvery   bell the kind of
Bell you see next to a sign that says *Please ring for service*
And you just stand there scared to ring it it   was sewn
To the top of his head   sounded like an elevator's
Bell   then he bent to the heated crank   it turned it seemed
More easily   the dusty rope it   was hanging where
The elevator should have been   the cab   the dusty
Rope wound around a steel bar just below the ceiling
A wooden bucket   after half an hour appeared
Attached to the rope at the handle   and the robot bird
Barked *Don't   you worry fuckface that's a double knot*
Get in it was   just big enough for us to stand in
What are you fucking looking   at that asshole for
The bellhop looked at me *Oh   it's a backward well*
He said *The bucket   goes down full and comes back empty*
But you don't want to hear my joke you want to ask
Me how I stand to turn the heated crank he   glanced
At Law gears whirred   in its thin neck as the bird nodded
The bellhop spoke again *Were you   familiar with*
The powers you served in life   I serve the pit I am
Grateful to know the fire   the painted crank is worse
Who wouldn't choose   instead of Hell eternal life
In Heaven   but I wouldn't want to suffer there
You suffer once in Heaven you will suffer always
Threatened by bliss unknowable because it's threatened
And trapped because how can you damn yourself away
I couldn't stand the threat of peace I couldn't have
It is a backward well   you lose your hope in it
He wept and chuckled as he cranked the bucket down

A Revelation of a Further Darkness

The laughing bellhop cranked the elevator down
Weeping   the walls of the shaft from no source glowed no spot
-light no projector blue with every chuckle green
With every sob the white   of the floating rocks that float
On Crater Lake forever dirty white of rocks
Floating on water   clean forever   the pitted walls
Glowed white with every gasp   from too much laughing too
Much weeping blue then green for hours   those alternating
Then white then   green then only white the light on the walls
In the middle of or maybe   near the bottom of
Or maybe really not so far from the top of the shaft
Although I couldn't or not me   and not the robot
Bird see from where in the shaft the walls began to only
Ever glow white no blue no green   I couldn't see or
We couldn't see   the light at the mouth of the shaft and were
So deep we heard each gasp now only after each
Glowing the gasp occasioned   maybe Law   the robot
Bird could see farther up than me so maybe Law
Could see the light at the mouth of the shaft   but I don't think
Law could hear sooner no and later   in the dark
-ness so far down the shaft long seconds stretched between
Each flash of white and each faint gasp I asked and Law
Still couldn't see the bunker   no although by then
We swung in the bucket far   below the mouth of the shaft
So far   we only heard the   gasps we couldn't hear
The sobbing hidden in the light by which we saw

No One Goes in Whole or Comes out Healed

The dirt at the bottom of the hole the elevator shaft
Dug through the heart of the mountain or just naturally occurring
Or say what hole in Hell would not be natural there   what thing
In Hell or Heaven could be artificial   black or maybe
Brown but brown   mixed with blood a hot moist brownie or brown hair
Stuck to a bleeding head   the dirt in the darkness at the bottom

Glowed with a light that didn't rise I couldn't see the dirt
Unless I pressed my face so close to the dirt I couldn't breathe pre
-tend to   the light so bright I almost couldn't see the dirt
I turned my head to breathe   and saw the light was interrupted
By the elevator bucket ten   or fifteen feet away
A sudden black horizon where   from where the robot bird

Had when the bucket   finally touched the dirt had shoved rough past
Me clanking toward a glowing orange thimble shape in the blackness
It must have been a door   and far enough away it looked as
Small as a thimble calling   to it now the robot   Law
I turned   my head away from the bucket toward the glowing door
But saw no shadow stopping the trapped light   but only light

From where I knelt to the door   I couldn't see Law's feet   and now
I realized I hadn't since Law stepped from the bucket felt
The tug of the invisible cord binding us together
I stood and standing left the light and leaving it could breathe
And calling still   the bird's name shouting *Law* in Hell I walked
Half-stumbling   I expected I at every step might stumble

Over a rock or roots or over   anything since standing
I couldn't see the light that didn't rise from the dirt   I couldn't
See even my own feet in the light   that surely as I stared
Were passing through the light like fingers through an infant's hair
Both there and not there   shouting as I raised my eyes to the door
Again I saw   first at the heavy upper edge and then

At the center of my vision it the glowing orange door
It wasn't getting bigger it the thimble   wasn't though
I stepped I thought was   stepping closer though in the dark I wasn't
Sure I was moving though I saw the thimble slide from the upper
Edge of my vision to the center so I knew   my eyes
Were moving maybe with my head were moving   in the dark

The only things I knew for sure were moving were my eyes
In the dark in which I called the name of the robot bird named Law
Until not   ten steps after I had raised my eyes I slammed
Into a fleshy wall and saw the door between my feet
Or where I thought my feet might be and heard the whirring of
The brittle gears in the robot's neck beside me   to my right

And high above my head   a gray and blurry grainy noise
Law laughed   and laughing choked and coughed then spluttered
    into silence
Then wheezing barked *That door's the door   to the HR bunker fuck*
-face it's so small 'cause no one goes in whole or comes out healed
It's mostly assholes who think Hell's where justice happens   Hell
Is sorrow's Heaven where it goes   to live forever with

Its god the human body   that's why you're the dirt the walls
Not you but fuckers like you PEOPLE shit you stupid fuck
It doesn't matter what you understand   no human body
Fits through the door intact I gotta make you parts just then
I felt again the cord that bound me   to the bird but didn't
Feel the cord wrapped around my waist but like a fine net gripping

My body tight at many points   I heard the rusty gear
That turned whenever Law winked creak   loudly I felt the blade
-Sharp strands of the net   tighten through my body through my head
I fell through the net I fell through   quiet my tongue in parts I fell
Through meat I fell through   bones no blood the blood not dripping
    each
Part of me fell through sealed each wounded edge   I fell through
    seeing

Each wound an opened eye and clothed in the light by which it saw
Each glinted pink from the light   no longer trapped in the dirt but
    risen
Set free the instant I was sliced apart   to seal my wounds
My blood now trapped by the light that had been trapped in the dirt
    each part
Thumped in the dirt   Law pulled a red toy plastic shovel from
A slot above the door   and knocked me shining through the door

I squeezed through

the door between the field of light
    Of the trapped light between   the field and
    The HR bunker   as I rolled in
-to the cramped doorframe I was might

Have been   if living I was me
    And mine complete in every part
    My fingertips   my eyes my heart
If cut off   out   me still   a knee

-cap shattered and the shards like slivers
    Each tweezed from the   basin jagged pearls
    A treasure of myself   though curls
The wave as if it were the river's

Hair the river has no head
    No body   is no river but
    Its waves I might have been   was what
My parts had been alive   if dead

Not like the dead are dead but al
    -most half   -alive still   if in pieces
    And as the first piece rolling squeezed just
Barely squeezed through the door   a ball

Of marrow tightened by the squeezing
         Me squeezed and tightened   the other side
         Of the doorframe stretched away the tide
In which the river finds its being

Rolls far from where   the waves in which
         It finds its being meet the sea
         The doorframe stretched away from me
Became a hallway as it stretched

As more of me and   more and more came
         Through the unending door through   one
         Side of the door   and I heard then
Law barking in the walls   *The doorframe*

Between the field inside the mountain
         That   shithole and the bunker is
         The only part of Hell that is
-n't human isn't flesh   not counting

The girders sometimes in the skin
         'Cause even here the bones run out
         Nah   it's not flesh   the boss shits doubt
And that's the pipe   doubt comes out clean

In the HR bunker   bodiless
         So maybe that's the underside
         Of flesh it   isn't human I'd
Lie to you   sure but   not about this

You're the first solid doubt the boss

        Has had in years   a century

        Fuck if I know   shit   honestly

I've never been to the bunker gos

-sip and weird fucking looks   from demons

        Who say they know   demons who've seen

        The other side of the asshole   when

You get there so will I I'll   see then

Yeah fuck you I will see then Law

        Stopped talking   and the tunnel stopped

        Lengthening all   at once I dropped

All of me   dropped before I saw

The end of the tunnel   I was through

        Before I saw the end of the door

        The other   side of the door   before

I knew   I had   rolled glowing blu

        -ish white and fire   to the bunker floor

Law's Dream

dreaming is incompatible with freedom because
dreaming leaves us with no sphere of action
—Susan Stewart

I rolled in   glowing shreds like sparks through the thimble door
And I beheld *beheld's*   the only word for it
I saw but now I'm writing it it   might be helpful
Since anyone can die
                    since it might help the dead

And that's still helpfulness right sure it is   advice
To the disincarnate that's still help I rolled   the many
Glowing with the freed light the many   shreds of me
Strained through the net
                    that bound me to the bird that *had*

Bound me the bloody   shreds were free the way the light
That clung to them was free released but with a purpose
I rolled through the door and in the HR bunker glowing
Bloody beheld my purpose
                    saw with every shred

Of me as if my skin and guts were eyes   suspend
-ed from the ceiling must have been the ceiling was
Hanging on wires   from something too high up to see
A giant screen
                    divided into many screens

A monitor electric glowing hanging maybe
Fifty a hundred feet above a forest of
Gray cubicles impenetrable loud from which
A storm of static
                              but the storm was screams arose

An endless forest   like a wall but I could see
The boundary of each cubicle in front of me
A wall in parts each hopeless as an endless wall
Each closed no anywhere a window door
                                                         except

No roof on any on   the monitor I saw
In each a different torment different suffering
For what I guess each   for a different sin the screen
Expanding constantly
                              new cubicles appearing

New cables hissing down from the too-distant ceiling
As if the light on the screen got heavier with each
New sin   in each new cubicle   at first just one
Person the torment but then soon
                                                         another person

Sooner another one I watched the cubicles
Fill up the screams were   right away too loud for me
To hear them getting louder   I can't write down all
The pain I saw
                         in the first cubicle I saw

I saw as if the camera floated high above it
Swimming in later the bird told me molten copper
Law told me later men the   damned I saw were men
Jawless their faces partially submerged
                                        that

The copper poured through   them erupted from their backs
Having first burst their stomachs which were even as
They burst re-forming to be burned apart again
Law smiled
          describing what was happening inside them

The tightening of straps I took to be its smile
The men had when they were   alive through screens had
    threatened
And mocked degraded others strangers anyone
They could I saw
                in the first cubicle I saw

In the second cubicle I saw I saw a box
Tall as a coffin deeper than a coffin wide as
A phone booth phone booth deep   from front to back from where
Men entered it
              the   coffin vertical men entered

The coffin through the lid as if it were a door
One at a time a line of men I couldn't see
The back of the line it was beyond the boundary of
The cubicle
            but each   of the men I saw was wearing

A rubbery transparent business suit each floated
Through the door churning slow his legs and listlessly as
If he were running in his sleep or trying to
Away   from demons monsters men
                                    but couldn't run

As often in a dream some power confounds your will
And though you try to fight you feel your punches brushing
Weightless against the face of your opponent   inches
Above the dirt
                    each floated churning through the door

Each branded on his forehead and his cheeks with the name
The full name not   the friendly name of the large bank
And with his title at the bank   where he had worked
Each an executive
                    and in the box each screamed

Then a loud *POP* and out   the back of the box each suit
Floated   a pink mush dripping quietly inside it
Otherwise empty   its legs dangling   floated back
It must have floated back
                                    to the back of the line I saw

Whole again men returning helpless to the box
I looked to Law itself more box than bird   but also
It walked on legs that might have been a person's legs
If Law were flesh and were not steel
                                    I looked to Law

And would have spoken shouted but Law slapped a hand
Over my mouth I   felt at once my mouth again
My body whole again   Law turned to me and barked
While you watched two I watched them all

                            I'm watching still

Each cubicle each poor fuck shocked a hundred years
Of being shocked to be in Hell   a thousand years
Of being shocked   I'm smiling still but   shit you fucking
Dick you don't want to know

                   why you just want to know why

You don't see women only   men well you're a man
And it's the HR bunker Hell wants you to care
In Heaven you'd see men and women people who
Are neither   people who are both

                 but no   not you

No even when you're watching people being tortured
You gotta fantasize it's you   not just the poor
Fucks suffering either no   you gotta fantasize
The you who cares to watch them

                I have watched and seen

I'm smiling 'cause I know you recognize my smile I
Could hurt you   so you've learned my face   and   fuck I'm smiling
'Cause I know all the faces on the screen   I recognize
Even the torn-off faces

             lying flat in the dirt

I'm smiling 'cause I'm overfull   with faces wait
No Law   stopped barking and I heard the voice I now
Knew was the boss's voice first muffled grunting as
If it were wrestling in Law's chest with

                                        what and then

A CLANG a THUMP then panting then a scraping sound
The sound of   something heavy a thick stone lid being
Slid into place a marble lid   and then I heard
The voice again   Law's beak not moving   wide

                                        Behold

Each screen a petal of a flower both   rootless and
Eternal and you watching watch   as angels watch
The Earth   from their perspective yes you watch as though from
Above although you stand below

                            the special gift

I give your kind you   people   is perspective that's
What all that garden slander means   and see   I made my
Own tree of wisdom and of being alive   its petals
Ever budding spring

                        tree of one flower nonetheless

Diverse and more enfruited than mere trees FOR MAN
LAUGHS SOONER THAN HE LOVES   ESPECIALLY
    WHEN HE LAUGHS
AT OTHERS' HARM oh   I've got casks of wisdom wisdom
Pours from each flattened head

                        and reddens leaf and petal

Listen   I let you look around I could have claimed
You for my own at any time   I didn't have to
Capitulate I did   the Weary One a favor
Letting you tour the place
                              but now I see I shouldn't

Have given you a guide a   demon's better off
Attending to a single petal   Law was made
For a fixed world   the only multiplicities
A demon understands
                              are pornographic show

It growth and change as you have seen my garden grows
And changes and you show it the eternal justice
From which it draws its sense of purpose   is not rock
But water
                              and it changes to fill different forms

No thing on which to stand but where to go with thirst
A demon has no hole with which to thirst   to hunger
I should have warned the robot not to bring you here
And now it sleeps inside itself
                              and dreams and this

Is it its dream me talking   now   to you and you
I damn   to live inside Law's dream the   boss stopped talking
And when he stopped Hell stopped I looked   at the screen all
The images were still
                              I turned to Law and Law

Looked like a statue in an anime a steel
Memorial both too   ridiculous and too
Beautiful to be real   and looking close I saw
A light begin to brighten
                              the roof of Law's beak

The light the only moving thing in the dream   except
I could have   moved but watched   instead the edge of the light
Sliding across the roof of the beak first yellowing
The gray then
                        whitening the throatmost part of the beak

And then the middle then the tip the farther it
Moved the more still the torments   looked the more Hell stopped
Seemed stopped it was   a sign the dream was ending in
Law's dream   the end of punishment
                                        is the end of the world

The Dream at the End of the Dream

At the end of the dream the light exploded
The robot   bird the pieces of
The robot flew   each piece about
Twenty   or maybe twenty-five
Feet away burning each piece flew
Then stopped no   stalled I would have said
Froze but the stillness that arrested
The pieces of the robot's body
Was more an engine stopping all
Connected motion   stopping than
A river freezing and the river
Still moves beneath the stillness where
The water meets the air   each burning
Piece flew   then stopped   stalled for an instant
In the air   and for that instant seen
Together   they had flown in all
Directions each   piece the same distance
From the bird as every   other seen to
-gether they formed a sphere around
The hovering now   a hovering
Flame where the bird had been   a sphere
A halo a cage   the burning pieces
Of the bird's exploded body   stalled
Then flew together back   to the pulsing
Flame   and the bird was there again

At the end of the dream the dream continued
And in the dream the robot coughed
Then shook its head   then blinked   once   twice
A third time then it stilled its eyes
On mine   and then it ran to me ran
Past me   behind me   turned then shoved
Me   toward a tall and narrow like
A needle tall and pointed at
The bottom wider at the top
An oval window   at the top but
Too high for anyone to see
Through door a   needle door on the other
Side of the HR bunker from
The thimble door I   had in pieces
Rolled through for how long   now had I
Been in one piece again why   could
-n't I remember

the tall door
Looked like it was a hundred yards
Away but two   three steps and we
Were there another   we were through
And standing in a camera
Obscura on the peak of the mountain
On which I dreamed before   I turned
My head and saw the needle far
Away Law   gripped my face   and turned it
Back to the aperture in the wall
I squinted ducked   my head and looked

And saw a sky beyond the sky
I had   watched as I dreamed on the mountain
And saw a second mountain floating
In the thick sky   high above mine
Which after the bird barked *Hey fuckface*
What do you see I   realized was
The surface of the lake   that was
The gate to Hell   and on the higher
Mountain   above the lake I saw
Through the distorting water saw
Snow at the peak   the farthest snow on
Far mountains   and below it closer
To me the impossibly close stone and
The closer trees   and the trees seemed
To pull me   to the foot of the mountain
My eyes to the foot of the mountain my
Mind in the camera with my body
But also with my eyes   at the foot
Of the mountain   on the mountain's slope
Green grass grew   on the mountain's slope
And small white flowers with petaled stems and
Corollas made of thorns gray moths
The size of with   their wings extended
The size of dimes flew   drunkenly
From flower to flower   on the mountain's slope
Nearest the foot of the mountain   white
Snow   gray stone   green trees the colors
Of the face of the distant mountain close and
Small where the mountain met the dirt

I watched the gray moths stagger from
The petals and the thorns and as
I watched as time   as time before
Had slid from me began to slide
From me at   first I didn't hear it
But once I did   in the midst of the sound I
Realized I had heard but hadn't
Noticed the voice of the robot filling
The sky above the mountain filling
The sky-blank plain   at the foot of the mountain
Howling a long   approaching *Looooooooooooook*
UP you can't sleep forever you
Can't dream forever sooner or
Later the dream will notice you
Sleeping between its teeth you fucker
I only brought you here   to take you
Away from here   but first you gotta
Look and I looked   and saw myself
High on the mountain climbing and
The bird behind me flying and
Wherever I stepped   the ground wherever
I stepped   after I had stepped two or
Three steps away a piece of the mountain
Broke from the mountainside and flew
Into the sky   and sometimes I
Glanced back to watch a piece of the mountain
Rise but always I turned back
Quickly to face the peak   until
Finally I glancing back I saw

A void had opened up behind me
That watching from the foot of the mountain
I long before had seen   I saw
Me finally seeing it and saw
Me finally seeing   that the pieces
Of the mountain each   piece was about as
Big as a Honda Civic had
Arranged themselves   into a wheel
They looked together like a Ferris
Wheel but with no spokes   no hub
And the wheel turned around the axle
Of the line between the darkness of
The void and the   light of the day
The pieces of the mountain rolled
As the wheel turned   into the void one
By one   and disappeared   and as
It turned the pieces of the mountain
Emerged from the void one by one
And alternately burning or
Encased in ice   and burning or
Encased in ice each rolled to the apex
Of the turning wheel   and at the apex
Of the wheel instantly the flames
Died or the ice   shattered and fell
Away and each   piece of the mountain
Rolled with the wheel back down   I stood
I don't   know for how long I stood there
Watching the wheel   eventually I
Noticed the bird standing beside me

And listening from the foot of the mountain
I heard as if I stood beside
Us I said *What   the fuck is that*
And the bird   who now spoke as it
Had never spoken speaking not
Barking said *The   fire and ice*
Are you and I   and I and you
And each is each   we are the same
Rock burning and we freeze together
And burn and freeze beside each other
Separately also   neither when
We rise together nor when we
Fall separately do we know
Each other   neither in our sorrow
Burning   freezing   nor in our
Joy when we reach the peak and are
Released to joy   and so we burn
And freeze   forever on a wheel
That's Hell   we've been in Hell

                              when I
Was told to guide you through I wasn't
Told where to stop   the boss just wanted
Me gone   and in the bunker watching
New sin new punishment new sin
New punishment new screens   the big
Screen never   full but always filling
Watching   I felt both   filled and made
Empty both overfull and for

The first time   hungry desperate
To leave   a demon can't leave Hell
For real I wanted to leave Hell
For real   but you can leave   I thought
Maybe if we   ran through the door
At the same time   if it's a door
I thought I'd try I would   just take you
As far as I could go the both
Of us would go   as far as I
Could take you   toward the end of Hell
Through Hell   and now I think I can't
Go farther no   a demon can't
Go farther this   is the end   but look at
Me   I am what we are together
And though I watched from the foot of the mountain
As soon as the bird finished speaking
I saw as if I stood before it
I saw the bird transform   a bright
Silvery liquid metal rose
From the bird's joints and coated it
And as the metal thickened the
Bird changed the bird   transformed but not
Into a giant robot but
A person   but a silver person
Silvery like a mirror like
The T-1000   the same height
As me   and with my build and face but
Its features blurred together in
The mirror that made its features and

I only recognized my face
When our two faces were aligned
And otherwise I saw the bird
I mean   I saw myself and knew
It was the bird I saw   and watching
I saw   in its bright skin the mountain
Change shape   at first I thought the change was
The strengthening wind   carving the snowdrifts
But soon I realized the mountain
-side was moving   carrying
The bird and me to the peak I watched
The sky approach in the bird's skin
That was my skin   I watched the sunlight
Open as the light opens in
Movies when the gates of Heaven
Open and the light flooded over
The bird's bright shoulders and bright back
I watched the once   -steep incline gentle
As flowering   trees apple cherry
And lilac trees green   shrubs green grass
And a blue   narrow two   feet wide
A playing stream   appeared in the skin
That was my skin the trees and stream
Warping together and apart
As the bird swayed as we were carried
By the mountainside   and finally
I watched the mountain slow and stop and
I turned from the bird   to see the peak
And saw what I had seen in the bird's

Bright curving skin   but differently
Each thing in its own place and shape
Reflecting sunlight   casting shadows
Echoing from its place forever
Into the earth and heavens like
A hand between two mirrors   facing
Each other a bare empty hand
Alive between infinities
Each thing in its own shape the place and
Sun of an echo of the place and
Shade of the fading echo I
Saw on the green peak

                    but almost as
Soon as I saw the peak I felt
Myself   pulling myself away
From the peak   I fell away from the peak
I fell

        and turned my head away
From the aperture I turned around
To tell the bird what I had seen
And saw the peak   glowing on the door
Opposite the aperture
But upside-down I squinted   then
I would have shouted but   the robot
Bird clamped its beak   over my mouth
And nose and rising over me
Its back to the aperture began

Flapping its wings   so rapidly
I thought its wings would break   and flew
Backward through the aperture
Lifting me out of   Hell and into
The cold lake from the bottom of
The lake   out through a film a little
Like it looked   a little like
Brown plastic wrap but passing through
It felt like passing through a fog
Like when you're driving   home in fog
And feel like   you have never known
Your way in the most familiar part
Of the world you know   into the lake
The bird   still rising pulling me
Up through the lake even as the currents
Its wings made pushed me down its wings
Twisting to slice the water as
The bird   raised them then flattening
To push the water down and lift us
Both the bird lifted us from the lake
Into the now   dark sky its oily
Beak over my mouth   and hanging from
Law's beak I must   to anyone
Below me watching me I must
Have looked like what I was   a worm
That had like   the blessed dead been joined
To a great hunger in the sky

Acknowledgments

Thank you to my friends and to my family. And thank you to the editors and staffs of *At Length*, *BOAAT*, *Conjunctions*, and *LVNG* magazine, in which earlier versions of parts of this poem originally appeared.

The original version of "The Hell Poem" appeared in *The Gilded Auction Block*, published in the United States by Farrar, Straus and Giroux, and in the United Kingdom by Corsair.

"The Finger and the Ditch" and "Interlude: The Mind of Hell" previously appeared in *The World Is Wild and Sad*, published by Theaphora Editions.

"In a Dream the Robot Bird Tells Me How It Is I Am in Hell," "The Dream at the End of the Dream," and "The Reformation" previously appeared in *Cain Named the Animal*, published in the United States by Farrar, Straus and Giroux, and in the United Kingdom by Corsair.

Extra special thanks to Jonathan Galassi, Sarah Castleton, and Anastasios Karnazes.